# VINCENT VAN GOGH

Copyright © 1981, Verkerke B.V. All rights reserved.
Produced by V.O.C.-Angel Books, Leidsestraat 12, Amsterdam.
Design: Roon van Santen
Printed in Germany by Mohndruck, Gütersloh
ISBN 90 6560 041 8
V.O.C.-ordernumber 7017

# VAN GOGH

# VINCENT VAN GOGH

V.O.C. - Amsterdam

*At the back of the Schenkweg*                    *May* 1882

It is hard, terribly hard to keep on working when
one does not sell, and when one literally has to pay
for one's colour out of what would not be too
much for eating, drinking and lodgings, however
strictly calculated. And then the models besides.

... All the same they are building state museums,
and the like, for hundreds of guilders, but
meanwhile the artists very often starve.

Rijksmuseum Kröller-Müller, Otterlo

*The Weaver*                                           1884

I for my part often prefer to be with people who do *not even know* the world, for instance the peasants, the weavers, etc., rather than being with those of the more civilized world. It's lucky for me.

So since I have been here, for instance, I have been absorbed in the weavers ...

Those people are very hard to draw because one cannot take enough distance in those small rooms to draw the loom. I think that is the reason why so many drawings turn out failures. But I have found a room here where there are two looms and where it can be done.

*351*
Rijksmuseum Vincent van Gogh, Amsterdam

*A peasant woman gleaning*                                    1885

It is a good thing to be deep in the snow in winter;
in autumn, deep in the yellow leaves; in summer,
amid the ripe corn; in spring, in the grass; it is a
good thing to be always with the mowers and the
peasant girls, with a big sky overhead in summer,
by the fireside in winter, and to feel that it has
always been so and always will be.

*413*
Folkwang Museum, Essen

*A peasant digging*                                              1885

*Even* in this century, how relatively few among the
innumerable painters want the figure ... for the
figure's sake ... and want to paint the action for the
action's sake ...

   *I should be desperate if my figures were correct*
... I do not want them to be academically correct ...
I mean: if one photographs a digger, *he certainly
would not be digging then.* I adore the figures by
Michaelangelo though the legs are undoubtedly too
long, the hips and the backsides too large ... My
great longing is to learn to make those very
incorrections, those deviations, remodellings,
changes in reality, that they may become, yes, lies
if you like – but truer than the literal truth.

*418*
Rijksmuseum Vincent van Gogh, Amsterdam

I have tried to emphasize that those people, eating their potatoes in the lamplight, have dug the earth with those very hands they put in the dish, and so it speaks of *manual labour* and how they have honestly earned their food.

I have wanted to give the impression of a way of life quite different from that of us civilized people. Therefore I am not at all anxious for everyone to like it or to admire it at once.

All winter long I have had the threads of this tissue in my hands, and have searched for the ultimate pattern; and though it has become a tissue of rough, coarse aspect, nevertheless the threads have been chosen carefully and according to certain rules. And it might prove to be a real *peasant picture. I know it is.* But he who prefers to see the peasant in their Sunday-best may do as he likes. I personally am convinced I get better results by painting them in their roughness than by giving them a conventional charm.

*Self-portrait* 1887

What am I in most people's eyes? A nonentity, or an eccentric and disagreeable man – somebody who has no position in society and never will have, in short, the lowest of the low. Very well, even if this were true, then I should want my work to show what is in the heart of such an eccentric, of such a noboby.

This is my ambition, which is, in spite of everything, founded less on anger than on love, more on serenity than on passion. It is true that I am often in the greatest misery, but still there is a calm pure harmony and music inside me.

Rijksmuseum Vincent van Gogh, Amsterdam

*The pink orchard*                    *spring* 1888

I'm up to my ears in work, for the trees are in
blossom and I want to paint a Provencal orchard of
astounding gaiety ...

The air here certainly does me good. I would you
could fill your lungs with it; one effect it has on me
is comical enough – one small glass of brandy
makes me tipsy here, so that as I don't have to fall
back on stimulants to make my blood circulate,
there is less strain on my constitution.

*473, 474*
Rijksmuseum Vincent van Gogh, Amsterdam

*Peach tree in bloom*                    *spring* 1888

At the moment I am absorbed in the blooming fruit trees, pink peach trees, yellow-white pear trees. My brush stroke has no system at all. I hit the canvas with irregular touches of the brush, which I leave as they are. Patches of thickly laid on colour, spots of canvas left uncovered, here and there portions that are left absolutely unfinished, repetitions, savageries; in short, I am inclined to think that the result is so disquieting and irritating as to be a godsend to those people who have fixed preconceived ideas about technique.

*B3*
Rijksmuseum Vincent van Gogh, Amsterdam

*Pont de l'Anglois*                               1888

I brought back a size 15 canvas today. It is a
drawbridge with a little cart going over it, outlined
against a blue sky – the river blue as well, the banks
orange coloured with green grass and a group of
women washing linen in smocks and multicoloured
caps.

Rijksmuseum Kröller-Müller, Otterlo

*Boats on the beach*                    *June* 1888

My dear Theo,

I am at last writing to you from Saintes-Maries on the shores of the Mediterranean. The Mediterranean has the colours of mackerel, changeable, I mean ...

Now that I have seen the sea here, I am absolutely convinced of staying in the Midi, and of positively piling it on, exaggerating the colour – Africa not so far away ... I made the sketch of the boats just as I was going to start in the morning, very early.

499, 500
Rijksmuseum Vincent van Gogh, Amsterdam

## The Zouave

*June* 1888

I have a model at last – a Zouave – a boy with a small face, a bull neck, and the eye of a tiger, and I began with one portrait, and began again with another; the half-length I did of him was horribly harsh, in a blue uniform, the blue of enamel saucepans, with braids of a faded reddish-orange, and two stars on his breast, an ordinary blue, and very hard to do. That bronzed, feline head of his with the reddish cap, against a green door and the orange bricks of a wall. So it's a savage combination of incongruous tones, not easy to manage. The study I made of it seems to me very harsh, but all the same I'd like always to be working on vulgar, even loud portraits like this. It teaches me something, and above all that is what I want of my work.

*The postman Roulin*                    *August* 1888

I have just done a portrait of a postman. A Socratic type, none the less Socratic for being somewhat addicted to liquor and having a high colour as a result. His wife had just had a child, and the fellow was aglow with satisfaction. He is a terrible republican, like old Tanguy. God damn it! What a motif to paint in the manner of Daumier, eh!

*B14*
Rijksmuseum Vincent van Gogh, Amsterdam

*Sunflowers*                                    *August* 1888

I am hard at it, painting with the enthusiasm of a
Marseillais eating bouillabaisse, which won't surprise
you when you know that what I'm at is the painting
of some big sunflowers.

   ... Now that I hope to live with Gauguin in a
studio of our own, I want to make decorations for
the studio. Nothing but big flowers. Next door to
your shop, in the restaurant, you know there is a
lovely decoration of flowers; I always remember the
big sunflowers in the window there.

   If I carry out this idea there will be a dozen
panels. So the whole thing will be a symphony in
blue and yellow. I am working at it every morning
from sunrise on, for the flowers fade so soon, and
the thing is to do the whole in one rush.

526
Bayrische Staatsgemäldesammlung, München

*Night café*                    *August* 1888

In my picture of the 'Night Café' I have tried to express the idea that the café is a place where one can ruin oneself, go mad or commit a crime. So I have tried to express, as it were, the powers of darkness in a low public house, by soft Louis XV green and malachite, contrasting with yellow-green and harsh blue-greens, and all this in an atmosphere like a devil's furnace, of pale sulphur.

Rijksmuseum Kröller-Müller, Otterlo

*Van Gogh's house at Arles*          *September* 1888

Enclosed ... a sketch of a size 30 canvas
representing the house and its surroundings in
sulphur-coloured sunshine, under a sky of pure
cobalt. The subject is frightfully difficult; but that
is just why I want to conquer it. It's terrific, these
houses, yellow in the sun, and the incomparable
freshness of the blue. And everywhere the ground is
yellow too ...

The house on the left is pink with green shutters,
I mean the one in the shadow of the tree. That is
the restaurant where I go for dinner every day. My
friend the postman lives at the end of the street on
the right between the two railway bridges. The night
café I painted is not in the picture, it is to the left
of the restaurant.

The sense of tranquility that the house has brought
me mainly amounts to this – that from now on I
feel I am working to provide for the future, so that
after me another painter will find a going concern. I
shall need time, but I am obsessed with the idea of
painting such decorations for the house as will be
worth the money spent on me during the years in
which I was unproductive.

*543, 540*
Rijksmuseum Vincent van Gogh, Amsterdam

*Olive orchard* *autumn* 1889

The olive trees are very characteristic and I am
struggling to catch them. They are old silver,
sometimes with more blue in them, sometimes
greenish, bronzed, fading white above a soil which
is yellow, pink, violet-tinted or orange, to dull red,
ochre. Very difficult though, very difficult. But that
suits me and induces me to work wholly in gold and
silver. And perhaps one day I shall do a personal
impression of them similar to what the sunflowers
were for the yellows. If I had had some of them last
autumn! But this half liberty often prevents me
from doing what I nevertheless feel I could.
Patience, however, you will tell me, and it is really
necessary.

*608*
Rijksmuseum Vincent van Gogh, Amsterdam

*Road with cypresses*                    *May* 1890

I have a cypress with a star ... a night sky with a
moon without radiance, the slender crescent barely
emerging from the opaque shadow cast by the earth
– one star with an exaggerated brilliance, if you
like, a soft brilliance of pink and green in the
ultramarine sky, across which some clouds are
hurrying. Below, a road bordered with tall yellow
canes, behind these the blue *Basses Alpes,* an old
inn with yellow lighted windows, and a very tall
cypress, very straight, very sombre.

On the road, a yellow cart with a white horse in
harness, and two late wayfarers. Very romantic, if
you like, but also Provence, I think.

## The Reaper                                    1890

Work is going pretty well – I am struggling with a
canvas begun some days before my indisposition, a
'Reaper'; the study is all yellow, terribly thickly
painted, but the subject was fine and simple. For I
see in this reaper – a vague figure fighting like a
devil in the midst of the heat to get to the end of
his task – I see in him the image of death, in the
sense that humanity might be the wheat he is
reaping. So it is – if you like – the opposite of that
sower I tried to do before. But there's nothing sad
in this death, it goes its way in broad daylight with
a sun flooding everything with a light of pure gold.

Rijksmuseum Kröller-Müller, Otterlo

Do you know what I think of pretty often, what I already said to you some time ago – that even if I did not succeed, all the same I thought that what I have worked at will be carried on. Not directly, but one isn't alone in believing in things that are true. And what does it matter personally then! I feel so strongly that it is the same with people as it is with wheat, if you are not sown in the earth to germinate there, what does it matter? – in the end you are ground between the millstones to become bread.

The difference between happiness and unhappiness! Both are necessary and useful, as well as death or disappearance ... it is so relative – and life is the same.

Even faced with an illness that breaks me up and frightens me, that belief is unshaken.

| | |
|---|---|
| 1853 | Vincent van Gogh born in Groot-Zundert, The Netherlands |
| (1857 | His brother, Theo van Gogh, born) |
| 1880 | Studied art in Brussels, supported by Theo |
| 1881-85 | Lived in The Hague, Nuenen (with his parents) and Antwerp |
| 1886-7 | Lived with Theo in Paris |
| 1888 | Moved to Arles in Provence. Gauguin came to stay. Attacked Gauguin, and cut off own ear |
| 1889 | Entered asylum at St. Rémy near Arles because of sporadic attacks of insanity |
| 1890 | Increasingly depressed. Moved to Auvers. Commited suicide 29 July. |
| (1891 | Theo died in January) |

# ACKNOWLEDGEMENTS

Published here are extracts from letters written by Vincent van Gogh mainly to his younger brother Theo. Two (*Peach tree* and *The postman Roulin*) are written to Emile Bernard, a painter, friend and admirer, and one (*Road with cypresses*) to the famous painter Gauguin. We are grateful to the New York Graphic Society for permission to use their English translation of the letters which was published in 1958 under the title *The Complete Letters of Vincent van Gogh*.

The numbers at the bottom of each page refer to the letter in this collection from which the extract comes.

V.O.C. GIFT BOOKS CAN BE ORDERED
FROM:

Great Britain: Verkerke Limited
Broomhills Industrial Estate
BRAINTREE Essex CM7 7 SQ

U.S.A.: Verkerke Reproductions USA Inc.
49 Walnutstreet
NORWOOD N.J. 07 648

Canada: Verkerke Reproductions of Canada Ltd
217 Richmond Street West
TORONTO M5V 1W2